IN THE CIRCUS OF YOU

IN THE CIRCUS OF YOU

An Illustrated Novel-in-Poems

Poems by
NICELLE DAVIS

Artwork by
CHERYL GROSS

Rose Metal Press

2015

Rose Metal Press, Inc.
P.O. Box 1956
Brookline, MA 02446
rosemetalpress@gmail.com
www.rosemetalpress.com

Library of Congress Control Number: 2014958496

ISBN: 978-1-9416280-0-3

Cover art by Cheryl Gross
Cover and interior design by Heather Butterfield

This book is manufactured in the United States of America and printed on acid-free paper.

For Louis and Harley, the two men in my life, and for my grandmother Ceil who taught me to be self-sufficient and strong.

—Cheryl Gross

For Jonathan Hughes and Curtis Thornhill. And for J.J.—always J.J.

—Nicelle Davis

Table of Contents

III. The Clown Act

IV. Beyond the Three Rings Is the Circus My Selves Dream of

INTRODUCTION

Go!
No you go!
Go!
You!

Two kids on the edge of something, egging each other on. To jump, to plunge, to flail and survive. We all know the power of being in cahoots. That sweaty hand in your sweaty hand makes the possibly-dangerous possible.

So it is with some collaborations. So it is with Cheryl Gross and Nicelle Davis. The bravery of one encourages bravery in the other. And the more they work together, the more risks they take, trusting that in concert they will make clear both what's at stake and how that risk can be understood. As Davis says, "Having an artistic partner makes searching in the dark fun instead of scary—well, at least it makes scary feel fun."

The poems and art of In the Circus of You teach us how to understand poetry and art. They demonstrate reaction and interaction. While the poems of In the Circus of You address the dissolution of a marriage and its aftermath, the art of this book addresses the inner creatures that prowl beneath our daily actions and reactions. They illustrate the psyche of the speaker and the situation.

When I interviewed Gross and Davis in 2014 for a feature in *Alaska Quarterly Review*, Gross said of her first encounter with Davis, "I got the same feeling as if I were encountering both Henry Darger and Walton Ford. It was as if I came home, so to speak." Darger and Ford, though worlds apart, make sense as iconic figures for Davis and Gross, because, in the words of Davis, "[they] do not mistake 'natural' for easy or 'organic' as lacking tension."

Henry Darger's desperately imagined fantastical world of strange, rebellious, innocent, pan-/non-/cross-sexual creatures. His rough, raw, urgent, dreamed reality. Walton Ford's crafted, hungry beasts, vividly realized with technical precision. Yes. That is the sense of the world that Davis and Gross create together in this book.

Davis ranges, in her poetry, through various forms and voices: short poems, prose poems, quatrains, experimental forms, near-concrete poems. The self wriggles to escape them all. However, the images created by Gross stay true to the intense reality of the self. Because Gross' artwork has such a distinctive line, Davis can deviate as much as she needs to in tone and persona. She is a tender mother, she is a prescription-pill rejecter, she is a woman reclaiming herself. The art grounds us and reminds us: this is *one* self. This is *one* vision and story, only possible through the two visions that have created it.

The parallel stories of destruction (of a marriage, of a self) and creation (of a grotesquerie of inner figures, of a new self) drive the book and amplify it. While the poems might move toward reconciliation, the art never backs off; the frisson of presentation and deep self are exposed. As Davis writes, "Conjoined with twine, bones of the first arrange with this new / pigeon. Two heads. Four wings. Gorge- / ous arrangement of lines. I make from them a necklace."

Davis and Gross seem to have always been a pair, working together. However, there is a beginning. In 2010, as editor of Broadsided Press, I received a submission over the transom from a writer I didn't know. The piece was a prose poem by Davis about teaching writing to disadvantaged students, questioning the value of focusing on sentence structure given the very real difficulties of their daily lives. It was raw, powerful, crafted, and surprising. We accepted it for publication and sent it out to artists associated with the press, including Gross: "Here's a poem we want to publish, who would like to respond visually?" we asked.

Gross wrote back within an hour: "'Composition 101' *sings* to me. I think it's right up my alley. Where do we go from here?"

From there, Davis and Gross have gone far. They have used that first contact as a launching pad for a strange and risky voyage, and now, with In the Circus of You, we are able for the first time to see more than a glimpse from that trip. We are able to journey with them.

Enjoy the teeth, throats, pigeons, cannibals, and creatures of this book. Find yourself in the tender, cranky, confused, wounded, vicious mother/wife. Envision yourself as sword-swallower, sewn-up cello, punched door, exposed heart.

These poems and drawings remind us that our pains and triumphs are varied and glorious and wild. They will not be contained. Only in the crevices between image and word, knowledge and experience, art and poetry can the truth be found. Recognize your beasts here. Celebrate them. Let them loose and let them be transformed.

—Elizabeth Bradfield
Poet, and Founder of Broadsided Press

I. THE DAY-TO-DAY CIRCUS

I Drive Our Son around Every Day at Noon

I follow the dirt road to our rental, nestled between
a large horse corral and an empty pigpen. The hog has
been slaughtered; it waits in the yard to be buried
with a backhoe. Desert pockets every shadow—all
saturated in light, it's difficult to register distance.

The hog-head seems closer than it is, smiling ten yards
off. Sun on their backs, red horses burn as they round
the gate, passing trees ripe with crows. Fragments of
the hog lie beneath this orb of birds. I lift our son from
the backseat. His chest rising, collapsing, in time with
bird wings—sound of throwing knives—edges rotating
in air, without the treat of striking.

3

Gifts of a Shape-Shifter

You always want reasons for a feeling. I tell you to stop
yelling. You increase volume to show how far we are from
screaming. Sure. It could be worse. We know to follow
through with a punch. Make contact. But sometimes
the word *bitch* grows teeth. An all-hunger, cannibal name

to call me home, but I've mastered acts of disobedience. I
remain in wild poppy fields to herd fireflies into formation—
form a perfect ring of light by chasing my own tail. Round
to catch myself. Winning always smarts some. I return.

Panting over your chest. Early morning. You want to keep
sleeping. I want a different shape to fit my bones. *I'm not
a bitch*, I bark. Teeth nipping your ears. *Say I'm not. Not.*
The taste of blood. You want reasons for a feeling—

here are reasons: love's not nice, it calls me names—makes
a game of me. Makes me hungry and hurt where I've bitten
myself. I catch sight of us in a mirror—in my mouth a bird—
killed and gifted.

After a Fight

The cat curled at my center catches fire—light swells
in the kitten's red belly. Helium breath. Rising. My
throat dilates to ten. Charred creature crowns—purring.
Slab of meat falls from my mouth. Lands on its feet.
Blisters dragging towards you. Trail of fluid—cord
strung across the kitchen floor.   *...hell is that*
you ask, flying atop our counter. *Hope,* I say, but *Rope*
is what you hear. Bow of guts playing—nails down
a long chalkboard. *I think this Half-Gone likes you,*
I say. *Make it stop,* you say. I take it outside to roll
in the dirt—leave tuna cans at our door. The pet of
my innards paws the scent of sun-cooked fish. Shafts
of desert ground rise. Dust devils lift tumbleweeds
as an offering of matted sticks to indifferent air. I call
the cat back into my mouth.

On Its Haunches

the neighbor's poodle sits, a well-trained performer—
opens wide as lion's song. It shows me a place to rest
my head. Soft pink tongue. Trust, just another trick
to learn. On all fours, my face between teeth, I watch

children play in the street. They are eating bugs on
a dare. Worms raised above their mouths, they
patrol for each others' hesitation. None want to be
each. All demand others to act. Whole world con-

structed from match. If they make a show of sameness,
they'll beat judgment. It's the boy who wants this
least who goes first. No one follows. They laugh at him.
His mistake for believing. They leave him. *What are you*

looking at? he asks me. Kicks the dog. Yelp folds into bite.
My face is a circle of puncture. The boy calls me, *Freak.*
I turn red. *I'm telling your mother,* I say. He pulls incisors
out of the dog like scissors from a drawer. Cuts himself to

pieces. Re-grows as replica from every severed limb.
Which one of me will you tattle on? they ask in unison.
On the root of you, I answer. His multiples laugh at me,
You'll never locate our cause. Give it up, dog breath.

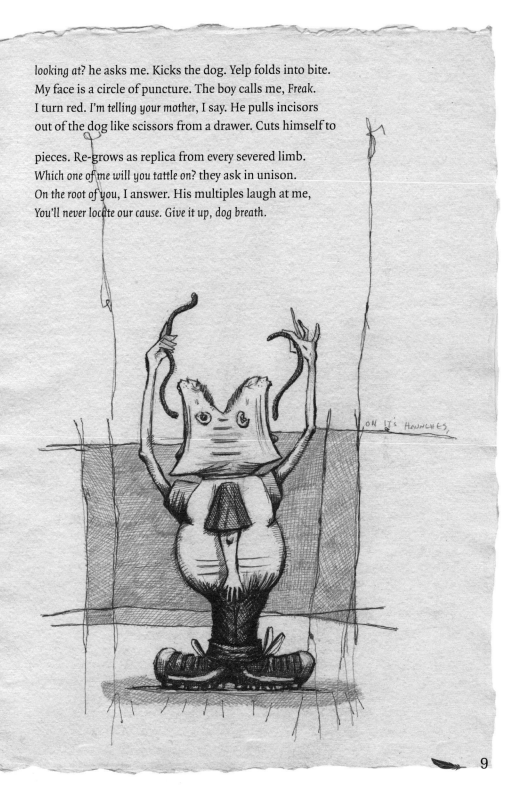

ON IT'S HAUNCHES,

9

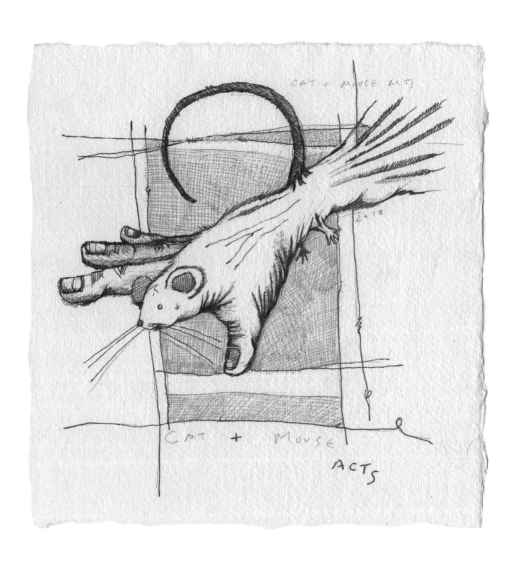

Cat and Mouse Acts

You taught your hands to move softly as thieving
mice, lifting the lids of my
eyes while I slept, so even my dream-self would
know you. Now there is
n't a night that can coax you into our bed, is
n't any of me that can
forget the cat-weight of sleep, pouncing.

In a Note Not Given to the Addressee

There is a hole the size of your fist in our bathroom door. My fault, I'm told, for pushing the hinge towards your movements. I used to dream of large machines with hands pounding apart concrete so a single seed could be sown. After this spectacle of effort, I'd wake with a fever of 103. You never understood how I could be sick so often. I do not feel well. Even without fever, I'm in pain—

an unseen pressure at the back of my throat, as though an egg-shaped stone were nesting in my swallow. I find comfort in looking through the door's injury. Through it, I see myself as a child resting in our bed. She holds a bird by its wings. The creature is tame as cut paper—its black eyes smooth mirrors, reflections of me in this hole. My child-self says to me, *The hole is. Not your fault. Not wholly.*

P.S.
You have installed a new door.

13

AGAINST ME   PRACTICAL THINGS PRESS

When Practical Things Press against Me

I snap like a fox at chicken thawing in the sink. It can be dead
again for all my teeth care. That insistent pecking. Sick of it.

Language of instruction delivered every first and fifteenth.
Paper bones want my red, but my birds are dead again already.

Carve my breast with a knife and bread it. Fry the feathers and
mail them first class to avoid late charges, but wings are slow

when dead already. I say, *Eat.* My boy says, *Old*—says, *Tastes
like dead already.* I say, *There is pizza on credit.* Credit says,

Red. I say, *My kid and pepperoni. Have my wings. Dead al-*
ready. *Take my other breast.* Another stamped fist of feathers.

I tell my kid, *After your head. After you run. They're after
your gizzards. So eat. Grow to blue. And don't ever come down.*

I've Decided to See the Physician

Where I am, sky pumps light like seeds through a thresher—
all bathed in the rusty colors of grain. Hard
to distinguish myself from this desert
that arches over my head and
recedes like the song
of Seraphiel.
Where I
am, a
constant
perdendo plays.
I don't want to disappear.
I want to feel my mouth on a hot
edge—to taste and know dark flavor—
separate from prayers spoken in genuflection against
you. Say Good-bye, Pigeon. I'm taking off our bones.

I'VE DECIDED TO SEE A PHYSICIAN

Dear Sir,

Please excuse my bird. It is impulsive and sings out of turn. I have seen a doctor. It's a frontal lobe issue. My gate is open. Always. Wings in and out of me. There are pills: Ritalin. Dexedrine. Cylert. My husband is relieved. Less stacking. More order. Less more. No letters without my knowing their exiting. [Pigeon caged] Doctor says it will still be me—only [[me caged better]]. Excuse how [(I love)] my impulsive feathers.

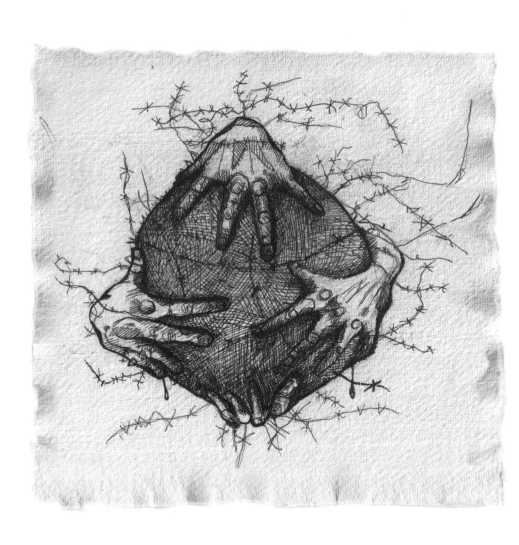

Wings inside Our Stomachs

I'm not a monster, you say. The little girl in me agrees—
sits next to your boy-self on the curbside
of our childhoods. I once believed the hole in you would hide
the girth on me, but combined
we are one jagged edge placed next to another. All rip and twin—
ball of barbed wire
passed between bloody fingers. We never meant harm—marriage
just was
n't our game. Would have fared better at monsters-in-the-dark—
we're
well practiced at running from shadows. Your boy-self can leap
a chain-
link fence with the weight of stolen guns in both pockets. My
girl-self can scale
selves—become a folded sheet to avoid a neighbor's "Doctor"
hands. Now, being found
feels like losing. Stop looking at me, and I'll stop looking
for you—omen. We're not yet tagged
into being what we've been winging so hard against.

Bought a Pack of Cigarettes Today

At this distance, street lamps are reduced to strands of Christmas
lights strung between windows
where televisions are erupting like fireworks from the eyeholes of
tract homes. A lit cigarette reflects
as a birthday candle off the surface of my windshield. Fighter jets
pass as the slowest moving stars—their
engines low moans—loud as breath in my ear. A semi-truck passes
as a streak of light chasing flight. Beneath me, red
ants are carrying the body of a black ant to their underground city.
If I didn't know hunger, I would think they were leading a funeral
procession. If I didn't know limitation, I would think the world
was in celebration of loss. It is
cold. Tonight. Please. Let me clarify.
I'm in an empty lot—next to a suburban neighborhood—alone
leaving you—
that is—three vacancies placed next to a thousand homes. When

I say
"a" cigarette, I mean "mine." When I say "my"
windshield, I mean "the car's."
There is distinction in ownership.
Guilt belongs to me. You gave me HPV, but I took it willingly—
wanting to believe in the religious alchemy of becoming one
flesh—put on cancer like relief. Impossible. Love. For me. There are
places in the sky untouched by shine. And this is what I focus on.
But must search for these rare absences between structures made
for together. Looking for dark

I catch sight of a couple making love in an upstairs window. The wind
is a torrent; I am wet from its intangible hands on my thighs. We are
done with each other. I recognize. I drove this far out of town to hide
from our son. Sometimes I choose cigarettes over tofu and sit-ups.

I understand my mother better at moments like these—know how she
could drag the body of a deer under her car for miles, because she had to

22

get away and needed all her available concentration to obey the directives of traffic signals.

Stop. Go. Slow.

I imagine the naked man in the window is being given direction. I have nowhere to go. Tonight is your turn with our family. Ours is a separate matter. You tell me I'm leaving too fast. I say,
I can't think right with the pain of my own teeth at my hands. I need to

stop eating cancer—
need to read books about spiders saving pigs to my son—
need to stop dragging a corpse every time I search for
a place to be. Quiet night. Birds
are sleeping in their twig cages built from the down of other birds. Harvested from bones. Their chicks blanketed in another's insulation. I long for

the friendship of morning, to see its red currents seeping through my closed eyes. To see myself divide. To have my shadow-self—
proportioned as a little girl with giant arms reaching for warmth. Again. I wish to make comrades of variance. Light and shadow never stop touching. Again. I flip a lucky. Spit the yoke of mucus. Wonder if this leaving will ever end.

Gravity

Pituitary gland: well the size of a pea at the base of the brain,
flooding my whole self in the wet rush of feeling. Rivers of fire
across channels of thought begin to form an image. The sun

is falling in orbs the size of grapefruit. Juggling these lights on
a high-rise ledge, I walk over the line of gravity. Phone rings.
I wake before knowing if what comes next is falling or lifting—

find your side of our bed empty. You've called to see if
the dresser and kitchen table are ready for you to pick up—
if *our* son has been split 50/50 by ink and paper cuts. *Sure,*

I say, fingers tracing the profile of *our* son in his bassinet,
rubbing *ours* from the brim of his nose. But the marks of us
refuse to come off—my eyes your mouth forever his. I pull

my feet over the edge of the bed, walk to the leaving table—on
the signature line, I sign *Gravity*. Then I begin to slice fruit into
halves—wet light in bowls of skin—to offer when you come.

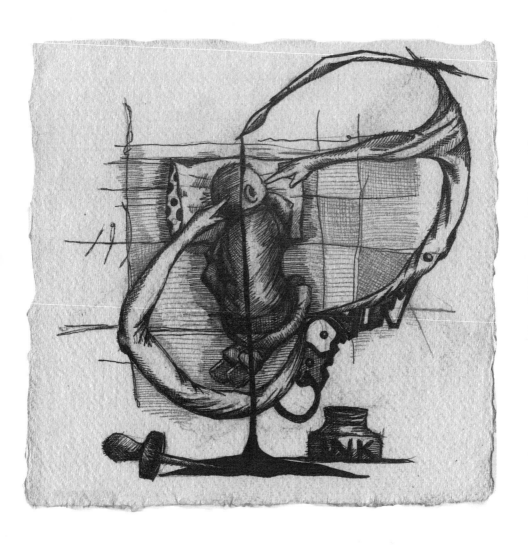

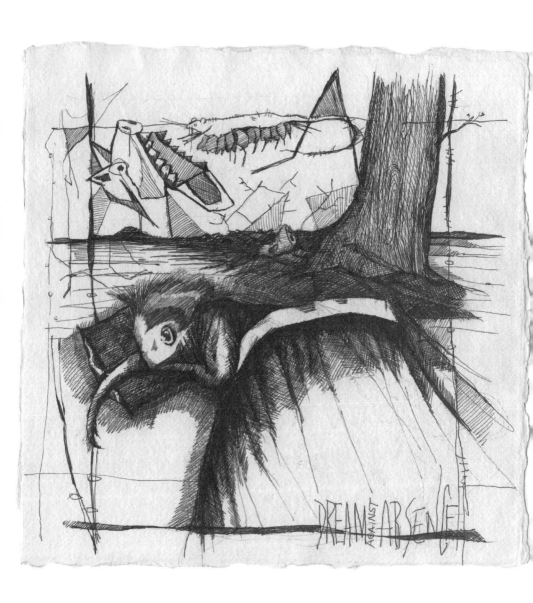

Dreams against Absence

I. First Night without My Son

I gather the scent of my husband like a bedsheet made of mice. Awake, the smell of our family scurries out from cracks in the walls. I cry this warmth made of little heartbeats—same as I cried for the empty womb once our child was born.

II. Second Night without My Son

My dreams are a mouse giving birth to a dozen pups. Blind and hairless, the rodents move slowly towards the scent of moonlight. Their bodies are open targets for crows, until the skull of the slaughtered pig opens its mouth and invites them safely in.

III. After Two Nights of Dreaming

At the foot of a tree, where the pig head was buried, I find a pile of gray feathers. The down floats towards me, as waves unfettered from the sea. A yellow beak the size of a diamond washes to shore. I push a thread through the breathing hole. Make a necklace of bones. At night I feel it roosting at my chest. I tell myself the wings were long swallowed, yet a palm-sized bird blinks against me.

Because I Want to Go Where I Can't

I lie face down on the ground—feel the earth shift with the movements of
an insect city beneath me. Their efforts to please a queen. She spends
her whole life spitting out colonies of search. When I die, I'll be
a present of flesh—a chance to appease another's hunger. But
not dead, I'm a mountain of pulse—a challenge for strings
of feet seeking until they can't. Tonight I'll dream
of can't—hinging open your mouth, making
a door of you. I'll reduce to the size
of an ant—find the taste of you—
sugar of someone's loss—
proportioned to the size
of a house. Finally
a place of effort-
less joy,
located.

A Secret Note from the Dream-Self

Search for the pig's head
blindly—with a spoon,
uproot the skull. Its empty
sockets house dream-
sight. Wear it. You'll see
the pulse of imagery.
Pictures occupy both living
and dead spaces—dreams
are made from such over-
laps. Make a ladder to
reach down the burrow of
your throat. Then trace
the sky's profile with a dry
tongue on parchment.
Rungs are made from tran-
scribed birdsong, but
keep its melodies to yourself.
Dreamers risk a butchery
of words. A bone helmet is no
protection against what
they'll call you if they find you
inside a hog, singing
for the sky to dig you a tunnel
to the stars.

The Dead Messenger Pigeon Writes

I am made of bones and string. Bleached
and hollow. She doesn't like people
knowing about me. That is why
the rope. That is why escape.
My death was as your
birth. A warm wet
cylinder. A long
red passage.
I learned
your
language of arranged sticks from coyote's
stomach. I write you because I am
indebted. She gave my ghost a
skeleton to shake. I clank
it. She wouldn't want
you to know about
the excrement
—there was
excrement
involved.
But she
found
me
writing you now as a turn of favor.
She loves easily. And her loves
turn to fish. She is afraid of
the fish drowning, so she
knits them to the sky.
Her vision is tied.
Is tired. It can
't submerge
without
the sun
reeling

it back to shore. She only sees fear in
a knife, not potential. The fish want
to be cut free. Please send
an edge she can
't recognize.
Please don
't tell her
I can
write. She would be ashamed of the excrement. And
the bones. My bones. She wouldn't want you to
know   she is a   collector of bones.

Lunch with the Biologist

Nurture can only do so much. There are birds
who migrate the world plus some—others
who will be burned alive if their tree catches
fire. Some stay. Some can
't avoid movement. Half-done human embryos
resemble chickens. Do you still believe in rehab-
ilitation? If pricked, will you not stain this table
with the sins of your DNA?

Pigeon Says, *Beyond Our Genetics Is Love*

Sparrows will peck crows to save their
chicks—but it requires chasing
nightmares. Dreamer,
listen to the music
of their wish.
No getting
out
without
going in. The
songs of birds released
from their predator's crop is
a joy our hearts can't put words to.
Protect your son. He, like dreams, is you.

II. RECRUITING TALENT
FOR THE APPROPRIATION CIRCUS

I Know How to Bark (The and/or of Reality)

The better I get at barking, the more difficult it is
to realize pitch from product. It's not that I can't
recognize what a thing is—it's simply easier
to walk down dark alleys when their walls
are covered in stars. And why not. Dress
truth in feathers and rhinestones. And
while I'm at it—Unicorns. Un-
icorns who (are) like me.
First circus I ever saw
had such a creature—
horn drilled into
the skull of
a goat. I
knew
it was
fake from
the blood circling
the mount. But I chose
to see what the ringmaster told
me. I cried like a blind girl made to see beauty.

My Understanding of Love between Women—or— *La Macchina da Cucire*

is a show seen on YouTube. You watch
paper clothes stapled onto a naked woman
with an upholstery gun. Her mouth sewn
closed with a hand needle. In the back-
ground, string instruments strike dissonance.
A voice repeating *The body is dead*. But
you see her blink. Another woman acts
upon her. With each stitch you see them
unite. She is obviously in pain. Other-
she, obviously considerate of this pain. Each
flinches slightly at contact, but does her best
not to acknowledge the ins and outs of thread.

My Understanding of Love from a Man—or—
The Rubber Boy (born the same year as I, 1979)

A reconstructed text from Marc Hartzman's American Sideshow

Straitjacket routine done backwards—
he first did it to be cheeky—to lose his
job. Now, he is famous for escapes into
restraint: *The World's Only Living
Enterologist.*

Self Discovery: Age 4, he fell
from his bunk-bed and landed split
in half. Then books with pictures.
Contortion. Mimicry as hobby.

Final act: Dislocates hips and shoulders.
Carefully rearranges ribs. Drops heart
below sternum. So an audience can
watch it beating.

My Understanding of Love of Self—or—
What I Can Recall from the Film *The New Sideshow*

Lucyfire says,

I ask the audience if they want blood. Always
the answer is *Yes*. Until bleeding—
then they all yell
No, no.

The act in summary is this:

With a syringe she pours herself into a cup
and drinks. She makes this look like
hunger's first contact with
consumption—lips so
erect you can see
her mouth
pulsing.

Lucyfire says,

I had a normal childhood, maybe spent
too much time alone
with a book—
of matches.

LA SIRENA

What the Appropriation Circus
Teaches Me about Want—or—
Sideshow Serpentina:
The Last of the Split-Tailed Mermaids

The poster shows her bare-
breasted. Areola painted
pink on yellow paper,
a picture of heat, stage
lights focused on the wet
split of legs, one limb pulled
into the loops of the other.

Nickel crowds line up to see
the boneless woman. Un-
ossified, she lays a rag
draped on planks. A man,
taken by her inescapable
need, buys himself fresh
fish off the ice at market.

On the trolley, rolling
fingers over scales, he
feels her blonde curls.
Home, unwrapping trout—
newsprint damp, ink bled—
he hates himself for
thinking he could have

such shimmer,
            such silver.

Complications in the Art of Monogamy—or—Conjoined Twins

Sheets hung from lines block
the sight of a half-man in full
rapture. A wife wraps round her
side of a torso, her legs quiver
at climax. Clutching to the edge
of a bed, brother tries to quiet
his blind effort, bending to
the will of brother's movements.
Both undone in, tonight not his
woman. Blue morning clutches
his empty limbs. He falls asleep
to the soft coos of brother's bird-
song singing, *beautiful* into
the matted web of bride's hair.
Breath joining three to a rhythm
of one.

*

Sister died before her. The living woman refuses to be cut from the corpse. She says,
As we came together, so we go together. Dragging loose legs across the kitchen floor,
she puts a kettle on. Sipping hibiscus, she feels her sister's cold lips kiss their neck.

*

During sex, a conjoined twin will slip behind
        the consciousness of the other
to provide privacy. While searching his wife's
        living dust for the light kneaded there,
he grieves for the loss of his brother.
        The wall of flesh rises with cell
division. Wife longs for the hirsute feel

of her Wolfman ex-lover.
Every kiss begs to break bread—
        to have multitudes dwell together
in the pleasure of light upon light upon light.

★

Conjoined sister at thirty masturbates for the first time. The weight of her dead
sister draped next to her, she forgets the corridors of their limbs. Body overrun by
light. Desire shucked off, she moans the song of settling earth. Dusk covers her.
Alone and complete.

Ella Harper: Lessons in Accountability—or—Why Students Make the Best Teachers

Death unknown—the dash after her birth lends to the possibility that she's living off money she collected from being shown in 1886 next to lions and elephants. Billed as a quadruped—knees bending opposite—stage named *Camel Girl*. But it wasn't enough. Curiosity unsatisfied. Audiences felt cheated. She had no humps. In pictures she holds herself up by table ledges. Her face is soft as a child's, but her eyes solid as fists. She wants an education. I build a school for her—sepia paper doll. Use my teeth as a desk—my tongue for a chair—assign books—talk about sentence structures—how the misuse of grammar creates emphasis. More than any, she holds me accountable for staring. It is her shy smile—straight bangs— overbite that remind me, no matter how I've been called an animal, I've never had to fight a camera for human recognition that I am of their kind.

In the Office of Family Law, Mediation Day—or— How I Learned to Pity God(s)

The rug is a collection of triangles overlapping as scales on a fish, or dead birds
on stretchers, or stacked boxes, one wrapped surprise after another. My ribs kick
as salmon—lungs unable to keep up with currents of breath. A river runs over the
banks of my external. Stiff sparrows are soaked to their floors by my crying as I wait
for a chance to stamp mine on our child's forehead with something like ink, but it
all smells of blood. How to end floods I wonder—how to damn half a DNA—to be
completely one's own. Oh, poor birds—sentinels of heaven—
wet boxes full of fish.

The Lizardman—or—
A Question of Choice

Entire body tattooed in scales, tongue sliced,
horns cosmetically embedded under skin—a self-
made freak. He is married. He likes to eat pizza.
He describes his look as an artistic development.
He looks happy.

Opposites—or—
A Lesson in Wishing

He was a giant. She was born without legs.
They adopted children. Ran a vacation camp.
Their daughter recalls, *It was what everybody
wishes theirs was: no talk of divorce, no big
fights, no drinking, no smoking. Just a family.*

CHANGING STATION

The Woman I Would Most Like to Emulate—or—Joan Whisnant, Musician and Mother

Born without arms, Joan could change her baby's
diaper with her toes. Her parents, refusing to see
their daughter as a helpless girl, taught her how to
make beauty with her feet—cut paper dolls and
strum guitar chords. She wore love like a second
face—one she would offer to the newborn placed
beside her. Her look beneath this gift is how I
would carve marble—features of determination—
if I were asked to forge a statue of what I believe in.

The Postpartum Sideshow—or—
What Do I Know about Being a Freak?

Almost nothing. But. When my son was born I had flashes
of my kid-brother lighting himself on fire for attention—how
at six I shaved off all my hair to be seen. I didn't trust myself
with this armful of breath now outside me. I avoided edges
and sleep—stopped showering. All so I could watch him. And
watch him more. People called me crazy. I told them, *Come near
us and I'll take your face with my teeth—starting with your eyes.*

III. THE CLOWN ACT

As the Pill Is Taken

I. Your Prescription Is Normally Used to Treat Adult Bed Wetting

Swallow, Doc says. Sure it's not right, but it's what you can
afford and it will stop the mania by coating you
in warm wax. Your mind a candle.
Wouldn't you like that? A
flame concentrating
on the wick. The
rope. Wouldn't
you like to
be a single
cord tied
to what
fuels
you? Wouldn't you? Like that. And swallow. Down—

II. Messenger Pigeon Sends an SOS from the Plastic Sack of a Migraine Headache

The fish of your throat were teaching me to swim, so I might catch and eat them—
turn their flesh to breath, exhale sky—have them fall like rain to be
the light in their children's lungs, when I was caught in a net
of impenetrable skin. Sun hurt my bones. I had to resign
to darkness; had to stop living in order to be
alive. What are you doing? To us. Who
have loved you? Us. You cover
in blankets of constriction.
You should con-
sider: this
could be
all you
ever
know of dance. You. Who tie your own feet, hear this, I will not let Nots have you.

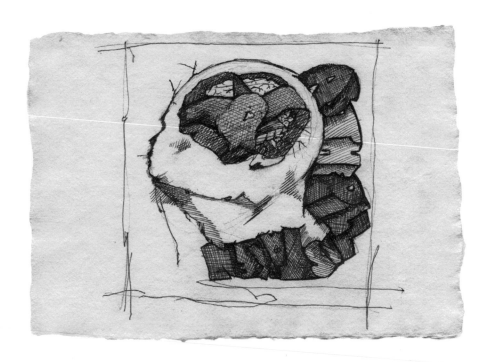

III. The Messenger Pigeon Waits For the Hole in the Plastic to Stretch

It is midnight and the moon will have none of this. Asleep you can't eat the can
't they feed you. I will take your left hand and carry it down
the portal of your opening. The dream tongue will
have you—suckle down like mother's milk—
yourself. You've been trained to
swallow. Now here is
the end of you—
turning inside
out. You
must be
led
by me—down your throat—towards light. An open window lives in you. Find it.

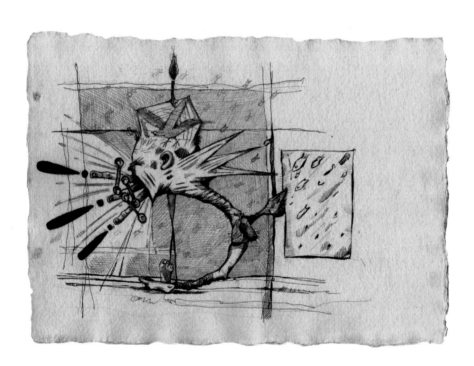

I Found My Own,
I Must Have Eaten It Not Knowing

This morning I woke as a sword swallower with my hand half-
down my throat. It took me an hour to gag it up. I couldn't
convince my fingers to loosen their fist. I begged. It knuckled,
knocking sound to my core. I shook from the impact. I had no idea

how sad the sound of me is, like starvation. Quiet. Teeth eating
their own mouth. That is my voice—music of a dull blade. And
I love it. This music. I stopped begging. Began singing. I felt
my hand start dancing—foxtrotting right out of me. Surfaced, I

saw it was holding tight to a poster. Wet, the ink didn't move—
paper hadn't weakened, as though it were a thing designed to be
nailed to the flesh of my interior. The wad, uncoupled from
its self touch, showed an image of a clown the size of my parlor.

Poster of a Clown

I crease the clown until he fits in my pocket, finger his edges and anticipate recon-
figuration. As my house sleeps, I open and close the folds like doors in
    a paper doll's mansion. Origami into a pool made of red
    tiles—I ride a white horse painted blue off a diving board.
We circle round Clown on his sinking bike. He pedals hard, pushing water
back—looks up from his cyclone asking, *Why have you brought me here?*
    I reply, *Dismount and buoy.* He says, *My foot has grown into*
    this machine, same as your hand has turned into a carrot.
The horse is eating my fingers—I wake to find my palm full of sunshine.
Approximation of touch. Sheets still smell of our marriage. On the night-
    stand, a photo of us on bikes by the sea. We smile at me
    alone in our bed. My lips twitch. I'd like to occupy my
mouth with chewing, but my fingernails are grazed to the quick. I've fallen
asleep in my clothes again—take from my back pocket the first love letter
    you ever wrote. Cursive like waves against the grain—as though
    a child has written a letter to the sea, asking to be saved from
the shore. I—wanting to be necessary as water—am a fool. To think. We
    could have been more to each other than drowning.

My Son Saves My Sight
from the Daydream Clown

I attach the poster with nails to my living room wall: the clown,
lit by my window, seems under spotlight—glow of celebrity.
I want to lick warmth from his lips, but fear teaching lust.

At the age of imitation, my son's a pirate's parrot on my shoulders;
I mean to show him how to read clouds, but the clown distracts me
with winking. In response my own eyes hatch into houseflies—

land where Clown's tongue can catch. My vision is nearly swall-
owed whole, when in a blink's time my son wings himself to peck
these insects—his cry regurgitating sight back into my sockets.

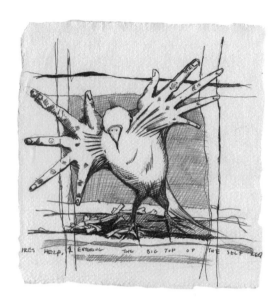

PRES HELP, I ENTERING THE BIG TOP OF THE SELF REQ

Entering the Big Top of the Self Requires Help

I. I Find a Second Messenger Pigeon Half Dead at My Door

Neck broken, attached by veins and skin, its head
lies atop talons—kicks its own face towards my
front gate. Incapable of flight, its wings reduce to
hands—fingers extending and retracting—trying
to escape pain. Reductive. Fistful of earth held in
feathers, it appears to be burying itself. I know to
spade its heart with a shovel. But can't. Not even
knowing *can* would end suffering. I watch it relax
and contract, as though it were giving birth to not.

II. An Above-Ground Burial

Wanting the bones but refusing the responsibility of flesh,
I cradle the bird in a box. Wrap the container in barbwire
to keep crows off, allow bugs in. Silverfish will make
bread of this pigeon until all that's left are pieces smooth
as the moon—confirmation that our centers are made
from a masonry of light.

III. The Message Brought in the Bellies of Silverfish

A blanket of silverfish covers me. They have learned to move
tonally—their tapered
abdomens rubbing together like words against clenched teeth
telling me, *Your kind-*
ness is monstrous. Life is more than the suffering you make it.

IV. Making One Necklace from Two Dead Birds

Conjoined with twine, bones of the first arrange with this new
pigeon. Two heads. Four wings. Gorge-
ous arrangement of lines. I make from them a necklace,
heavy as a baby's head against my chest.
With it on, I am a queen adorned. I order the silverfish to drop
from my body as a bodice undone. I stand
in a circle of exoskeletons catching glint off street lamps—
beneath me has become a carpet of stars.

V. Steps Begin to Swivel down My Throat

The two birds arch their wings to make a place for my left—
then right—foot. I begin the descent into the tent of myself.

Down the Trapeze of Bird Bones

The clown in my pocket breaks through my eggshell
pants, his eyes—sunny-side embryos—go down my
throat. I follow after, wrapping a naked leg around
pigeon ribs—fingers reaching for the spine and wings—
falling fast. There are flashes of red flesh and a man
laughing. I hit ground and feel full, as though a feast
has been fed to every empty mouth nesting in me.

The Clown in My Gut

tips his hat and hands me an inflated
snake—twisted to the shape
of a rose. Fangs mean
to bite, but I'm
saved by
rupture.
A dart
deflates venom before the flower can
catch my nose. Rubber skin
molts like confetti. You
win, Clown hisses
into my liver
where
my
younger-self crouches over her face—
cranium swaddled in needles. Pin
head, slurs Clown to sound
like In bed. Cradling
our detached
head like
a new-
born baby—she pulls a dart from our
eye—pops Clown into a million
blue balloons that exit
in the direction
from which
I came.

Clowns Promise What Can't Be Delivered

I empty the bottle of pills onto my kitchen-counter—
arrange them into smiling faces.

You said that these clowns were the solution to our
marital problems—that who I am

ruined *us*. Now clown faces are all over our house,
offering gags. Too many riding

in one car—(*you shouldn't have gone after that
other...*)—flowers throwing-up

their dinner (*...girl who was nothing like me*).
Shoes big enough to double

as rafts, (*When I bled...*) where a flood steals
the ground (*...in our bed...*) out

from under (*...you should have hoped for*)
their tripping over (*...the stain*) air

(*I miss myself more than I'll ever miss us*).
I'm done swallowing clowns.

IV. BEYOND THE THREE RINGS IS THE CIRCUS MY SELVES DREAM OF

What Became of My Younger-Self

She cuts her face into quarter slices and feeds them to her alligator
shoes. Her feet digest expression to make fertilizer for a garden
of snapdragons. Doing chores, her body's a modest storm—

stooping and standing, pruning and planting. Her long black dress
a backdrop to hands conducting an invisible army of song. The wind
singing for what is buried—calling what's been lost up from compost.

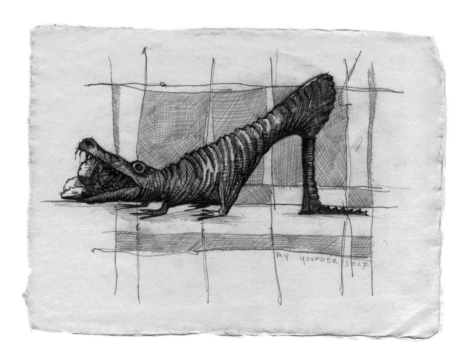

The Acrobatics of Snapdragons

A row of faces pile, one upon the other. When I pinch
their snouts, they talk as puppets for my former self—
her head splintered into a thousand blooms of color
speaking only in repetitions. *He loves me, if ripped
here—not love is the luck of even petals.* I pluck
until half buried in lady lips—pink slivers of skin
thrashing on the ground as trout pulled from a river—
drowning on air.

Riding Ponies outside the
Road of Constant Return

I find my faceless self weaving between ponies on a carousel.
Cannibals, the horses are furious at the poles that keep
them at bite's distance from each other. They can
't move faster than the gears of a music
box. Stepping onto the platform, I
hold my younger-self as
a mother might hold
her grown daughter, open
my mouth and a cage full of
birds fly as an endless strip of cloth
pulled from my center—a banner reads *Yes*.
Resolute, my younger-self feeds herself to a horse.
Paint turns to flesh—rides itself outside the circle—we are

no longer defined by limitation.

The Mob of Freaks Protests

We, like you,
are wrongly
used. Close
your eyes and
let us all go.

Brought Back to Life Inside-Out

Submerged, breath an intake
of fluid, held upside down, I
'm slapped, the bones of a bird
burst from my mouth and shatter
as pelts of water on the ground.

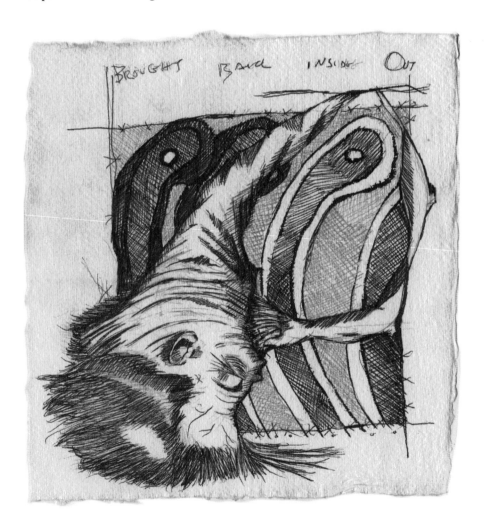

Reborn Inside-Out, My Life Is Explained to Me by My Six-Year-Old Son

Reborn for exposure, my body's been redesigned for uncensored
feeling: a sneeze or hiccup comes as a sheet of ice or a bed on fire.

Eyes inverted, the optic nerves reach like roots beyond me. I under-
stand the unseen scars of invisible knives—those rodents' teeth,

those crows' bills; natural insertions. The red of it is raw; the surface
glistens like sap gnawed out from trees—wounds that outshine even

the sun—these wet lights are my earthbound constellations. What is
left of me, my son walks next to on his way to school. He tells me he's

learned, *Where rain and babies come from*; he says, *It's all the same,
really*. Inside. Outside. He doesn't notice any difference. He says,

Race ya, and we run into a storm of babies—falling. Life absorbs
quickly as water into earth and all is an unstaged show of growth.

We will die, Mom, he says, *But like star-matter we'll regenerate. Why
do you think that is?* I ask him. *So we can find the joy in it*, he tells me.

Our story will happen again.

The Making of *In the Circus of You*

Like any sideshow, the more you gaze the more you become what you look at; if we are lucky, then we are all looking towards each other—we are becoming a little more human.

Illustrator Cheryl Gross feels at times we are living in a freak show. As a matter of fact, she feels this way a lot—always has, since she was a kid. Then at some point she was made to feel like a freak. She supposes her feelings of abnormality came from the fact that she had to conform in order to fit into society, but she realizes now that convention and rebellion are both part of survival.

Like Cheryl, in hopes of surviving the emotional trials of daily life, poet Nicelle Davis often turns to the freakish for comfort. She stumbled across the film *Freaks* (1932) as a kid and has been watching it ever since. Tod Browning's cult masterpiece offers the viewer this: "We accept you, one of us!" This simple phrase cost Browning his career, yet continues to afford us hope, social justice, and our strange humanity. It wasn't so much the words, but who he had deliver the lines that drove him out of Hollywood. Rather than using make-up and prosthetics, Browning hired real freaks. Audiences were appalled; *real freaks!* It was enough to make moviegoers sick; it was enough to make the average person behave like a prejudiced monster. Nicelle has viewed this film until it has become something more like memory than a movie. She watches to see how she is not, and then in hopes that she is, a "freak."

This mutual obsession with outsiders and so-called "freaks" has something to do with the word "real." It has something to do with the idea of "acceptance." At the heart of it, *In the Circus of You* is about our monstrous desire to be, as the freaks in *Freaks* say, "one of us."

To us, the idea of acceptance and exclusion are at the core of other-ing and the origins of *In the Circus of You*. We founded our own circus troupe with this project. We met through the publisher Broadsided Press, which puts visual artists and poets together to make literary posters that are distributed across the world. There is a great element of surprise in this process because poets can't anticipate what an artist will see in their words. We were in awe of how our images and poetry made a partnership that complemented and supported each other without muting or taming either one.

In the Circus of You is an intimate view of loss—the loss of love and the prescribed narrative. The images and poems were created spontaneously and simultaneously through a yearlong email exchange—the art became a sort of conversation between two women who were rummaging through the wreckage of their failed marriages. Together we discovered what remains after hopes and dreams are demolished. We created dreams and hopes unfettered by others' expectations of "normal" and "correct"—we found our own story (strange as it may be).

In many text and art collaborations, the illustrations assist the writing, with the visual art being more of an afterthought. This was not the case with In The Circus of You. The only way we can describe the sense of our collaboration is that it is as if we are two portions of a soul that, after a lifetime of searching, have finally found each other.

Cheryl was attracted to Nicelle's work because it is intense, truthful, and profound. As a seasoned illustrator, she has found herself in situations where when faced with a dark subject, people have a tendency to shy away. But she felt she could bring an aspect to Nicelle's work that would lure readers in and allow them to connect even though they may feel a bit uncomfortable. The end result would be to retain and enhance the grotesque without compromise.

Nicelle feels similarly: that without Cheryl, there would be no circus and what is life without somewhere to run to? Nicelle is of the mind that all things worth exploring are beyond words; it is the ethereal exchange of ideas—the escape into another world—that keeps us returning to the circus. Nicelle sees this as the pause before the aerialist plummets, the breath-beat before she is caught that has us on the edge of our seats. The show is just the time between jumping and being caught. She jumped, Cheryl caught, and we have been flying ever since.

The collaboration that created In the Circus of You is a testament to our shared hope that we are human and therefore never "normal," but that we are beautiful, too. We press rewind and replay; we watch for connections, we hope to connect with the larger story, we hope to connect with you.

—Nicelle Davis and Cheryl Gross

Acknowledgments

Kind thanks to the following journals and festivals for first publishing/showing poems and images from the *In the Circus of You*:

A cappella Zoo
"Sideshow Serpentina: The Last of the Split-Tailed Mermaids"
"On Its Haunches"
"Cat and Mouse Acts"
"A Secret Note from the Dream-Self"
"In a Note Not Given to the Addressee"
"Entering the Big Top of the Self Requires Help"

Alaska Quarterly Review
"What Became of My Younger-Self"
"I Found My Own, I Must Have Eaten It Not Knowing"

Awkword Paper Cut
In the Circus of You, a motion graphic

Berl's Poetry Shop, Brooklyn, NY, 2014
In the Circus of You, a motion graphic

Dinosaur Bees
"The Postpartum Sideshow—or—
          What Do I Know about Being a Freak?"

Contrary
In the Circus of You, a motion graphic

Fringe
"I've Decided to See the Physician"
"As the Pill Is Taken"
"Poster of a Clown"

Front Range Review
"Gifts of a Shape-Shifter"

JMWW
"Wings inside Our Stomachs"

The Mom Egg
"Dreams against Absence"

"Pigeon Says, *Beyond Our Genetics Is Love*"
"Lunch with the Biologist"

Mosaic Journal
"Clowns Promise What Can't Be Delivered"
"Dear Sir,"

Moving Poems, movingpoems.com
In the Circus of You, a motion graphic

The Nervous Breakdown
"I Know How to Bark (The and/or of Reality)"

PANK
"Gravity"
"My Understanding of Love between Women—or—
        La Macchina da Cucire"
"My Understanding of Love from a Man—or—
        The Rubber Boy (born same year as I, 1979)"
"My Understanding of Love of Self—or—
        What I Can Recall from the Film *The New Sideshow*"

Poesiefestival, Berlin, Germany, 2014
In the Circus of You, a motion graphic

Poetry Felix festival, Antwerp, The Netherlands, 2014
In the Circus of You, a motion graphic

ReVersed Poetry Film Festival, Amsterdam, The Netherlands, 2014
In the Circus of You, a motion graphic

VideoBardo International Videopoetry Festival, Buenos Aires, Argentina, 2014
In the Circus of You, a motion graphic

Wicked Alice
"After a Fight"

Zebra Poetry Film Festival, Berlin, Germany, 2014
In the Circus of You, a motion graphic

Special thanks to Liz Bradfield of Broadsided Press, for introducing us to each other and making it all possible.

About the Author

Nicelle Davis is a California poet who walks the desert with her son J.J. in search of owl pellets and rattlesnake skins. The author of two other books of poetry, her most recent book, *Becoming Judas*, is available from Red Hen Press. Her first book, *Circe*, is available from Lowbrow Press. Another book of poems, *The Walled Wife*, is forthcoming from Red Hen Press in 2016. Her poems have appeared or are forthcoming in *The Beloit Poetry Journal*, *The New York Quarterly*, *PANK*, *SLAB Magazine*, and others. She is editor-at-large of *The Los Angeles Review*. She has taught poetry at Youth for Positive Change, an organization that promotes success for youth in secondary schools, MHA, and with Volunteers of America in their Homeless Youth Center. Recipient of the 2013 AROHO retreat 9 3/4 Fellowship, she is honored to work as a consultant for this important feminist organization. She currently teaches at Paraclete and with the Red Hen Press WITS program.

About the Artist

Born and raised in Brooklyn, New York, **Cheryl Gross** is an illustrator, writer, and motion graphic artist living and working in the New York/Jersey City area. She is a professor at Pratt Institute and Bloomfield College.

Cheryl received her MFA from Pratt Institute. Her work has appeared in numerous films, TV shows, publications, and corporate and museum collections, including: The Museum of the City of New York, *The New York Times*, The Zebra Poetry Film Festival in Berlin, Germany, *Jimmy Stewart and His Poems*, *Circe*, and *Becoming Judas*, among others. She wrote and illustrated the novel *The Z Factor*.

A Note about the Type

The body text of this book is set in FF Quadraat. Designed by Dutch designer Fred Smeijers, Quadraat was originally created for the Quadraat design studio in Arnhem, The Netherlands, but was actually released by the FontFont foundry in 1992. Though it has a quirky, modern appearance, Quadraat draws inspiration from classic old style typefaces such as Garamond and Plantin.

Egyptienne, the display and folio typeface, was designed by Adrian Frutiger in 1956 for the Deberny & Peignot Foundry. It was the first new face designed for the process of phototypesetting. It is classified as a slab serif or "Egyptian" font, a style that became popular during the early nineteenth century that is now associated with advertising and industrialization. Egyptienne's design, with its thick strokes and brackets, was clearly influenced by Clarendon, a font that has been used prominently in circus poster design.

The title font on the cover is 5AM Gender, a free font that was designed by Andrew Galarza in 2004. 5AM Gender is a warm and charming condensed sans serif with no sharp edges; however, with its bold strokes and heavy vertical stress, it makes a strong statement on the page. It gives the cover the feel of a modern circus poster design in the way that Davis and Gross' book takes old ideas and images from the circus and makes them new.

—Heather Butterfield